About The Author

Boddhisatya Tarafdar is an MBA and a post graduate in Mass Communication. He is a banker by profession however, he also devotes his free time for studying about Indian history and the history of Indian Freedom Struggle with special emphasis to the contributions made by Netaji Subhas Chandra Bose and his Indian National Army. He also propagates these facts to others by organizing quiz competitions, seminars with the help of his friends and by writing blogs. He is also a columnist and a passionate documentary film maker.

'Jai Hind'
'Jayatu Netaji'

I dedicate this book in memory
of my grandfather
Late Dr. Benimadhab Tarafdar
'Dadu, tomay janai pronam'

For your valuable feedback you may contact me at

tarafdar1@gmail.com
history-that-matters.com (for my blogs)
@boddhisatya (twitter.com)

Acknowledgements

'Ya Devi Sarva Bhuteshu Shakti Rupena Samsthita
Namas-Tasyai Namas-Tasyai Namas-Tasyai
Namo Namaha'

The life and the contributions of Netaji has always been a great inspiration for me and the same inspiration encouraged me to write this book. The divine presence of my parents, *Shri Bijoy Krishna Tarafdar* and *Smt. Krishna Tarafdar* - has been the greatest boon of my life. Their blessings also motivated me to take-up writing.

Bahitro, my son, who is just more than 2 years old, my pride and joy. He has just started reading and writing a bit. I really cannot wait and eagerly waiting for him to read my books. *Pragya,* my lovely niece, who is 5 years old and already showing expertise in her studies. I hope she doesn't find my books boring.

I thank my wife *Sangeeta* especially for bearing with me, as I could not give her time even on holidays due to my studies and research for writing this book after the hectic banking duties on week days. She showed good spirit and supported me in all my creative ventures. I know that this project has already occupied a special place in her heart. And, lastly my sister *Moumita,* who has always been a source of oxygen all throughout my life and a great source of inspiration. She has not only supported me for doing something creative but also showed me the path by her critical analysis. I am sure, she will be very happy seeing this book published.

I would also like to thank all my friends, relatives, well-wishers and my colleagues for their continuous support.

CONTENTS

PREFACE

Chapters

1) Beginning of a New Era
2) How They Occupied

3) Freedom Movement in India

4) World War II & India

5) Activities in Far East

6) "The Land of Buddha"

7) Deshnayak Subhas

8) The Great Escape

9) Arzi Hukumat E Azad Hind

10) War of Independence

11) Liberator of India

Preface

First of all I extend my heartiest thanks to you for picking up this book. This book is about the struggle and sacrifices made by the army men of the _Indian National Army_ or the _Azad Hind Fauj_ during their armed struggle to liberate India under the charismatic leadership of 'the patriot of patriots', 'Deshnayak' _Netaji Subhas Chandra Bose._ This book is the result of my years of study about the history of Indian Freedom Struggle and I have been studying books written by eminent historians, experts and researchers related to this field. From my detailed studies I could clearly understand that our history text books in India do not narrate the clear picture of entire Indian Freedom Movement and history must be rewritten to make the Indians and the world aware about the whole picture of our freedom struggle. I have heard eminent historian *Maj. Gen. G.D Bakshi* on various TV shows that the INA was fighting against the colonial British for liberating India and more than fifty percent of the total men of the INA had scarified their lives fighting the British. So how can we say that we achieved freedom of by the virtues of 'Ahimsa', 'Satyagraha' or 'non-violence'? I also believe that the 'non-violent movement' was really significant in India but merely mentioning the names of the brave revolutionaries of India and just stating about the formation of the INA by Netaji and having just one or two pages about their contribution will not do justice to our history of freedom movement........at all. Why should we be unaware about the whole story of the *Santhali Movement,* about the *Indigo Revolt,* why the text books do not narrate us how the *sanyasis* and *fakirs* raised a revolt against the colonial powers? And, why we should not have an analytical study about the life and the journey of Netaji Subhas Chandra Bose whom Mahatma Gandhi termed as *'the patriot of patriots'* and about establishment of the **Govt. of Free India** and the **Azad**

Hind Fauj. What we need is not merely mention the facts but also to make the students understand the significance of their contribution to liberate India. In this book I have not assessed these matters, which I believe I am yet not very much capable of doing, but I tried to very briefly narrate the story of the freedom struggle of the INA led by Netaji.

1

Beginning of a New Era

"Never lose faith in the destiny of India. There is no power on Earth which can keep India in bondage. India will be free and that too, soon"

- Netaji Subhas Chandra Bose

On August 18, 1945, three days after the Japanese surrendered to the allies, the Indian nationalist leader and the *Supreme Commander* of the *Azad Hind Fauj* **"Netaji Subhas Chandra Bose"** took a flight to Tokyo (or may to the Soviet). He was worshiped by millions and many were prepared to give their lives for him. He confronted the colonial British powers on the battle field and his only aim was to throw the colonial masters out of India. But his flight never arrived at its destination and the plane crashed near the Taipei airport and Netaji died....or so the official version goes. India and the world got to know about this news five days after the accident had occurred, as the Japanese news papers reported the same. Later in independent India, there were three commissions setup to investigate the death of Bose. Two of them reported that he died in the plane crash however, the last, *Mukherjee Commission* stated that the plane crash never happened. Many of us in India believe that Netaji did not die on that day and we still do not

know what has happened to Netaji after 18th of August 1945. But that particular day certainly brought an end to the "armed struggle" launched against the British Raj in India by Netaji's *Azad Hind Fauj* or the *Indian National Army*.

Later in 1956 when the former British Prime Minister *Clement Attlee* was on a two day visit in India, he stayed at the Governor House in Kolkata.

The then Chief Justice of the Calcutta High Court *Justice P.B Chakraborty*, who was also the acting Governor for the state of West Bengal at that point of time, had some detailed discussions with the British Prime Minister on various issues. Justice Chakraborty later wrote a letter to the publisher of the eminent historian *R.C Majumder's* book *"A History of Bengal"*. In this letter he stated that *"My direct question to Attlee was that since Gandhi's Quit India Movement had tapered off quite some time ago and in 1947 no such new compelling situation had arisen that would necessitate a hasty British departure, why did they had to leave?"* Chakraborty added *"In his reply Attlee cited several reasons, the principal among them being the erosion of loyalty to the British crown among the Indian army and Navy personnel as a result of the military activities of Netaji."* This conversation was first published by the *Institute of Historical Review* by scholar historian *Ranjan Borra* in 1982.

It is noteworthy that Clement Attlee was the Prime Minister of Britain from July 1945 till October 1951 and during his tenure the Indian Independence Act was passed in British Parliament. Now we need to consider a few important points or a series of events which had happened during the *Red Fort Trials* by the British Govt. against the INA officials. During the proceedings of the trials the media in India for the first time got opportunity to cover the stories of supreme sacrifices made by the INA men under the leadership of their Supreme Commander Netaji Subhas Chandra Bose in the battles of the far east and not only they were fighting against the British-American allies but also against the problems of no air cover, limited ammunitions, almost no food to eat and no medical facilities. Now for the first time people of India came to know about the heroics of the INA and the contributions of the people of Indian origin living in various parts of entire East Asia and their struggle to make their motherland free. The INA officials could establish the point that this revolutionary army was governed by an established government in exile and which was recognized as a government of free India by nine independent countries and being Indians they have all the right to fight against the colonial power to make their motherland free. And, no other pledge or oath is as greater as to fight for the freedom of your motherland. As the British authorities had literally arranged the plot of Red Fort Trials to bulldoze the INA and treat them as traitors after the end of World War II, it resulted as a serious embarrassment to them. Anger irrupted among the people of India and demonstrations and processions started in the entire country in support of the INA men. Meanwhile after the war, the authorities demobilized or decommissioned nearly 2.5 million Indian Army men (of the British Indian Army) and they were even not entitled to get pensions. These events created a huge anger and mistrust among the armed forces in India against their British masters, whom they have served for centuries as a loyal force. As eminent historian *Gen. G.D Bakshi* in his path breaking book *"Bose: An Indian Samurai"* mentioned that *"the INA trials had inflamed the Indian soldiers, sailors and airmen of the British Indian Armed Forces."* The first revolt was seen in the Royal Navy, around twenty thousand sailors in twenty shore establishments had revolted and the pulled down the Union Jack and hoisted the Tricolour flag. They refused to obey their British officers and marched in the streets of Mumbai and Karachi with the portraits of Netaji and shouting his name and other INA slogans such as "Jai Hind", "Chalo Dilli" and then the agitations started in the Air Force, where according to Gen. G.D Bakshi, the signalers had spread on wireless the INA trial related news and coordinated the revolt. Finally the mutiny was seen in the army units in Jabalpur and this was the final blow to the colonial masters. Due to the heavy protests in all over the country and the revolts in the armed forces the authorities had to release all the INA officers and other soldiers. This was enough for the colonial masters to understand that time has come to grant independence to India as this has become very difficult to control the armed forces, which were loyal to them till then and they will not be able to handle an 1857 like revolt any-more. On 20th February 1947 British Prime Minister Clement Attlee announced that the British Govt. would grant full self governance to India by June

1948 at the latest. Netaji's prophecy after the defeat in the war proved to be true, that when the Indians would be aware about the sacrifices of the INA and the Indians of East Asia, they would revolt against the colonial British and that will pave the way of their exit. Now the statements made by Clement Attlee to Justice Chakraborty about the role of Netaji and his men in granting freedom for India may be better understood.

However, in India we have never learnt our history in this manner. We have always read that we have won our freedom mainly due to soft powers of *ahimsa*. But we should not forget the contributions of our revolutionaries along with the non-violent movements. More than fifty percent of the INA men have laid down their lives fighting for their motherland, nowhere in the world in the history of warfare we could find such an example. The last big movement launched by the Congress was the so called non-violent Quit India Movement during World War II, which was successfully demolished and crashed in 1945 by the British authorities by using the armed forces from Australia and New Zeeland. Therefore, during 1946 this was the final effort made by Netaji Subhas Chandra Bose and his INA that made the colonial British bound to leave India. There is no doubt that the non-violent movement was very significant in the context of Indian freedom movement however, we must give due credit to the efforts of the revolutionaries and the efforts of *"Desh Nayak"* Netaji Subhas Chandra Bose, who was regarded as a hero and a symbol of freedom and revolutionary ideas in the entire East Asia. So, history must be re-written to make people aware about all the aspects of our history, more precisely our freedom struggle.

Netaji had great ideas for nation building but at the beginning of a new India, Indians did not have their beloved leader with them. In 1947 we had seen communal riots and finally the great Indian subcontinent was divided into two dominions, India and Pakistan on the basis of religion. This was certainly the beginning of a new era.

"Deshnayak", *"Patriot of Patriots"*, **Head of the Govt. of the Azad Hind and the Supreme Commander of the INA, Netaji Subhas Chandra Bose**

<u>2</u>

How They Occupied?

"We should have but one desire today- the desire to die so that India may live- the desire to face a martyr's death, so that the path to freedom may be paved with the martyr's blood"

- Netaji Subhas Chandra Bose

There are many people who are of the opinion that the British created the idea of a political union called *India* and provided the tools and institutions needed to hold the union together. However, we need to keep in mind a few points that the concept of "Bharatvarsha" was mentioned in the epic of *Mahabharata* and Bharata or India was described as a single cultural entity. Under the emperor Ashoka in 300 BCE, large parts of the subcontinent enjoyed cultural and administrative unity. On the other hand, 200 years colonial rule did not unite the Indians, instead, they took every possible step to divide us, so that, it becomes easy for them to rule us. The Hindu caste system became more rigid and the communal lines between Hindus and Muslims deepened during British rule in India. Their cruel taxation system destroyed Indian economy and made Britain rich enough to prosper and rule a large portion of the globe as *British* colonies. Railways, post offices were established so that this large country may be properly administered by them and not for the welfare of the native Indians. We experienced the massacres like *Jalianwalabag* and deaths of millions of Indians in the man-made famines during the rule. Finally, at the time of leaving India the colonial masters partitioned the Indian subcontinent on communal lines in to India and Pakistan.

So, how the Britishers colonized India? *The East India Company* or the *Company Bahadur* or simply *The Company* was a British joint stock company, formed to trade in the Indian Ocean region. Finally, the Company ended up seizing control of a large part of the Indian subcontinent and colonized parts of South East Asia. The Company received a Royal Charter by the British Crown to operate trade activities in the Indies. Initially the focus of the Company was on trade only and not on building empire in India. But its intentions turned from trade to politics or more precisely in capturing territories during the eighteenth century, as the Mughal Empire declined. After the winning the *Battle of Plassey* by defeating the *Nawab of Bengal,* the Company got the right to collect revenues from Bengal and this was a major breakthrough by them in gaining control over the Indian subcontinent. By 1803 the Company had a private army which was almost double the size of the British Army. With the help of this private army which mainly had native Indians, the East India Company captured large portion of India and effectively started ruling India. However, their rule lasted till 1857, when the *Indian Rebellion of 1857* happened. This was an uprising in India by a large section of the native Indian sepoys, against the rule of the Company. This was a major revolt also known as the first movement of Independence in India. Though the revolt was ultimately crushed by the Company by 1858, but this resulted in the British Crown assuming direct control of the subcontinent and this was the beginning of the *British Raj* in India.

Robert Clive of British East India Company with Mir Jafar after defeating the Nawab of Bengal Siraj-ud-Daulah in the Battle of Plassey in 1757

==

<u>**3**</u>

<u>FREEDOM MOVEMENT IN INDIA</u>

"The roads to Delhi are many and Delhi still remains our goal. There is no power on earth that can keep India enslaved. India shall be free and before long."

- Netaji Subhas Chandra Bose

A large area of the Indian subcontinent as a single administrative unit was seen during the *Mauryan Empire* in 322 till 185 BCE, then in *Gupta Empire* and during the *Mughal Empire*. And, finally we see the same during the *British Empire*. The concept of *Bharata* or *India* has evolved as a symbol of *unity in diversity* for various reasons, which includes a mixture of rich cultural heritage, religious aspects and practices etc., which was highly evident during the glorious Mauryan Era and Gupta Era. In the medieval period, during the rule of Mughal Emperor *Akbar*, India regained its cultural glory which was destroyed due the attacks by the hostile rulers or invaders from *Turkey, Mongolia* and *Afghanistan*. Akbar rationalized the taxation system, discontinued the unfair *Jizia* tax (which was about levying tax on the Non-Muslim subjects by the Muslim ruler), he established alliances with the Hindu Rajput states and with other local kingdoms. Akbar helped India to regain its old glory with a secular fabric into it. The Mughal Emperor *Aurangzb* on the other hand, had destroyed the secular fabric, he re-introduced the Jizia tax and intensified persecutions of the Hindus, Sikhs and Bhuddhists, destroyed temples and also engaged himself in unnecessary warfare. All these events resulted in revolts among the Sikhs, the Marathas and in other provinces and finally led to the decay of the Mughal Empire. The *British East India Company* took full advantage of this situation and they systematically recruited sepoys, trained them on European methods and created a large infantry based army, which helped the Company to conquer virtually the entire India. The Company colonized India and in the name of good governance started a systematic loot of the colonized land and its people. This was accompanied by racial discrimination and fake supremacy attitudes on the part of the colonial masters. They destroyed the local craft and industry and pushed their machine-made products. They cut the thumbs of the weavers of Dhaka who used to weave the famous *Muslin* cloth. The Company forced the farmers to cultivate opium and *indigo dye* for trade other than cultivating food crops like rice. All these actions generated great outrage among the masses. In 18th century Bengal witnessed a great uprising against the rule and laws of the *Company Bahadur*. The Hindu

Sanyasis and Muslim *Fakirs* together started the famous *Sanyasi Vidroha* or the *Sanyasi Rebelion.* Modern India's first novelist *Bankim Chandra Chatterjee's* novel *Ananda Math* written in1882 is based on this *Sanyasi Vidroha.* The song *Vande Mataram* was published in this novel, which later became the mantra of Indian Nationalism and in free India, the song was given the status of the national song. *Santhal Rebellion* of 1855 was a major event in this regard, when the people from the Santhali tribe of the eastern Indian region bravely revolted and fought against the British and the local Zaminders, who were supported by the Company. In 1859 Bengal experienced Indigo Revolt or the *Nil Vidroha* by the indigo farmers, against cruel laws of the Company. All these rebellions were demolished by the Company with the use of its infantry power. Then the East India Company suffered a major blow when a large chunk of its sepoys revolted against them in 1857 and this is known as the *Sepoy Mutiny.* The mutiny started in Bengal, and then it became a full-fledged rebellion in Meerut. After that it spread over almost all over India. However, due to lack of proper coordination and lack of leadership the revolt could not be properly carried forward. The East Indian Company ultimately crushed the uprising by using brutal force. But it shook them to their roots and *British Govt.* took the decision to take direct control over India. That was the beginning of *British Raj* in India when Indians became the subjects of the *British Crown.*

Santhali Rebellion

An indigo factory in Bengal

Sepoy Mutiny of 1857

Indian novelist Sahitya Samrat *Bankim Chandra Chatterjee*, who gave Indians the revolutionary mantra for freedom *"Vande Mataram"*

Gen. G.D Bakshi in this book explained that the British Raj declared the Poorbiya (Eastern) troops of UP, Bihar and Bengal with the help of which they had conquered the bulk of India, as non-martial and stopped their recruitment into the British Indian Army. Then the British started recruiting Sikhs and Punjabi Muslim men, who had largely remained loyal to them. A large number of *Gurkha, Kumaonies, Ghar-*

walies and *Dogras* were recruited to keep the people of the Indo-Gangetic plains under check. The British Indian Army was raised on the ethnic parameters so that the concept of *India* is erased from the minds of the army men and the only idea which will strike their mind is about being loyal to the British Raj. Emphasis was given to build regimental system based on ethnic and linguistic identities.

The British adopted every possible way to divide the society that might be on the basis of religion, caste, language or ethnicity. We all are aware that to weaken the *swadeshi movements* in Bengal, the Governor General *Lord Curzon* tried to divide Bengal on religious lines in two parts in 1905. But protests erupted in whole of Bengal against this move. The intellectual class of Bengal also joined the movement in their own ways. *Gurudev Rabindranath Tagore* wrote the famous patriotic songs *"Ekla Cholo Re"* and *"Amar Sonar Bangla"* (the national song of Bangladesh) at that point of crisis, which generated great strength to the protest movements. *Ekla Cholo Re which* means "go your own way alone" became the theme of anti British movements in all over India. This song

Gurudev Rabindranath Tagore was a poet, story writer, novelist, song writer, composer, actor and painter. He was the first Indian, first Asian and first non-European to receive the Nobel Prize. He was also a great educationist and implemented traditional gurukul style of teaching with the blend of modern education in his school Viswa Bharati, Shantiniketan. He motivated the Indians with his patriotic songs to stand tall against the colonial British. He renounced the prestigious 'Knighthood' title after the infamous Jallianwala Bag massacre. Songs written by him "Jana Gana Mana" and "Amar Sonar Bangla" are the national anthems of present day India and Bangladesh. He termed Netaji as "Desh Nayak" and Gandhi Ji as "Mahatma". Netaji Subhas Chandra Bose was a great admirer of Tagore and adopted the Hindustani version of Jana Gana Mana "Subh Sukh Chain" as the national anthem for his Azad Hind Govt.

is often quoted in the context of any political or so-cial change related movements even in present day India. *Mahatma Gandhi* was deeply influenced by the song and also cited the song as one of his favourites. In 1911 the British Government had to change their decision and Bengal was reunited. The caste system was a curse in the Hindu society however, the first caste based census of India began during the British period, which gave an official recognition to this cruel system. The aim was to divide the Indians so that, it becomes easy to rule them without any hindrances.

The *Indian National Congress* was founded in 1885 by *O.A Hume* and *W.C Banerjee* was the first president of it. The Congress party's aim was to politically represent the Indians and in later years the party took active role in the freedom movement and fought against the colonial British mainly through the non-violent protests. *Mohandas Karamchand Gandhi* an Indian lawyer from Gujrat, who generated huge impact during the anti British movements in South Africa, returned to India and joined the Congress Party. Gandhi with his principle of non-violent tactics, *satyagaha* and mass civil-disobedience became the greatest mass leader for the Indian people and a huge hurdle for the British Raj. Gandhi was the person who orchestrated the freedom movement in the 30's and early 40's with the help of other Congress leaders like Gopal Krishna Gokhle, C.R Das, Dadabhai Naoroji, Lala Lajpat Rai, Bipin Chandra Pal, Bal Gangadhar Tilak, B.R Ambedkar, Sarojini Naidu, Dr.Rajendra Prasad, Maulana Abul Kalam Azad, Pt. Jawaharlal Nehru and others. The role of the revolutionaries throughout India were no less, many of them have given their lives for the sake of freedom for their motherland and many were imprisoned for long periods in various places and in the *Kalapani* or the Cellular Jail in the Andaman Islands. Shahid Khudiram Bose, Surya Sen, Binoy-Badal-Dinesh, Bagha Jatin, Chandra Shekhar Azad, Bhagat Singh, Rajguru and Ashfaqulla Khan were among the great revolutionaries that India had at that time. Poets and writers like *Tagore, Bankim Chandra Chatterjee, Kazi Nazrul Islam* contributed in the movement with their writings and speeches as a tool for political awareness among the masses.

Young *Subhas Chandra Bose* who was from an affluent Bengali family of lawyers, passed the exam for the ICS or the Indian Civil Services to fulfill the aspirations of his father but did not join the prestigious job and he joined the Congress party to fight the colonial masters. Bose became the President of the party on consecutive two occasions however, he had to leave the party as his revolutionary ideas did not go well with the then other top leaders of the party, especially with *Mahatma Gandhi*. By then with the help of his charismatic leadership style, his revolutionary ideas and his dedication to make India free, Subhas had already become a mass leader and *Gurudev Tagore* termed him as the *Deshnayak*. At the time of the World War II, Bose could successfully escaped to Kabul then to Germany through Russia to seek political help and to mobilize and assemble the prisoners of war Indian soldiers of the British Indian Army so that he can march in to India with the foreign help to through the

Mahatma Gandhi
Netaji Subhas Chandra Bose was the first person who
called him the "Father of the Nation"
The Mahatma said about Subhas that he is "Patriot of Patriots"

colonial powers out of India. Finally, he went to the Far East and with the help of Japan he formed the *Azad Hind Govt.* in Singapore in 1943. By then he became the beloved leader of the Indians in East Asia, whom they called the great leader or simply "NET-AJI". Netaji Bose's *Indian National Army* or the *Azad Hind Fouz* began war against the British Empire in India through Barma. However, after initial success the INA could not advance as the allied forces took control over the war by the late 1944 and Japan surrendered after the atom bomb blasts in Hiroshima and Nagasaki. It was end of the war of Independence for the INA men and in the mean time Netaji had gone missing after the plane crash in Taiwan and the reports were stating that he was dead. The last message by Netaji to his men was that though this war has ended but the road to Delhi are many, when the people of India would know about the sacrifice of the INA and the Indians of East Asia, they would revolt against the colonial British and they no longer can keep Indian in bondage. This prophecy became true and when the INA men faced trials, this caused mass protests and there were revolts in the armed forces.

On 15th of August 1947 ultimately India achieved freedom from the British Empire.

A rare photo of a paper cutting of The Hindustan Times at the time of India attaining freedom

4
World War II & India

The aspect of *Second World War* was a strange chapter in Indian history. The war which continued from 1939 till 1945 had left its deadliest marks on mankind not only in India but in the entire world. India at that time was under the British colonial rule and the whole of Indian subcontinent and its people had no connections at all with the war. But the colonial masters made the Indians fight on their behalf and the Indian men fought bravely at various battle fields of the world and gave their lives at the command of their British masters. The Bengal province witnessed one its worst disasters in the form of the **Great Bengal Famine** during WW-II. The famine took the lives of around 3 million Bengalis and remained as an infamous example of man-made devastations.

A picture of British Indian Army during 2nd World War

Indian Troops in Burma during the 2ⁿᵈ World War

British India officially declared war on Nazi Germany in September 1939. The Britishers, as a part of the *Allied Force* engaged around 2.5 million Indian volunteer force to fight under their command against the *Axis Powers.* The Indian soldiers of the British Indian Army fought bravely with distinction throughout the world and more than 87,000 Indian soldiers gave their lives in this devastating war. In the political sphere in India the *Muslim League* supported the war efforts of the British however, the largest political party in India i.e the Congress party asked for complete independence of India as a precondition before forwarding any support. Britain rejected the proposal from the Congress party and continued to send Indian men to the war front. As a result of this, Mahatma Gandhi announced the *"Quit India Movement"* in August 1942, which was the final movement demanding the end of British Raj. After the failure of *Cripps Mission,* Mahatma Gandhi made the call for *Do Or Die* in his Quit India speech delivered in Mumbai on August 1942. This was a massive mass movement launched by the Indian National Congress. The colonial government took the matter very seriously and within a short time they arrested almost all the top Congress leaders and there was no one left to lead the movement. The Muslim League, the *Hindu Mahasabha,* the *Communist Party of India* and most of the princely states of British India did not support the movement. At the end due to lack of leadership the movement lacked proper direction and there were occasions were the peaceful protests tuned violent. The government crushed the movement with the use of heavy force and armed forces from Australia and New Zeeland were also used for the same. Many people died due to the firing by the armed forces during the demonstrations and the movement ultimately failed. Importantly, in 1939 the president of the Congress party *Subhas Chandra Bose* after winning the presidential elections for the second time suggested Ghandhiji and the top other Congress leaders to start a armed struggle against the colonial British. He was in favour of taking advantage of the WW-II and throwing the colonial masters out of India with the use of force, which may require foreign help too. Mahatma Gandhi and most of the Congress leaders had different ideas and Bose had to leave the party. Shubhas Chandra Bose founded a new political party of his own in 1939, which is the *Forward Bloc.* Later when Subhas Bose went to Germany and formed the *Azad Hind Fauz* and in 1942 when Mahatma Gandhi announced the Quit India Movement and called for *do or die*, Bose through his *Azad Hind Radio* extended his support. Historians believe that though the ideologies of both Bose and Gandhi were different on the point of use of force but their thoughts came closer during the World War, as Mahatma called for *do or die.*

Quit India Movement

The Bengal Famine of 1943 is the name of another aspect of man-made devastations during the colonial British period or during the World War II which caused the death of nearly 3 million people. People died due to starvation, malnutrition, malaria and due to lack of medical facilities. During the period from 1942 till early 1943, military and political matters combined with the influx from Burma caused huge tress on the overall economy of Bengal which was mainly based on agriculture. Bengal had huge military deployment at that time which had resulted increased food requirements. The government was anticipating a Japanese invasion via eastern border of Bengal and the British destroyed the costal transportation system, so that, the potential invaders did not get access to food supplies, transport and other resources. But the economy of Bengal suffered a lot due to this reason also. Nobel Lauriat Economist *Prof. Amartya Sen* narrated that the main reason for the famine was the inflation that was caused due to the policies adopted by the British Government as according to him there was no shortage of food articles at that point of time. Huge stock of food articles was created to facilitate the war requirements. The required relief could not reach the needy poor of Bengal and the stock was kept to support the war related requirements at various places of the world were British Army was engaged. Importantly, the Viceroy of India *Archibald Wavell* recommended for stoppage of export of food from Bengal in order to use the same for famine relief. However, the then British Prime Minister *Winston Churchill* dismissed the request and even went on to state that *if the famine was so horrible then why Gandhi had not yet died of starvation.* Churchill also refused to accept the free relief materials for Bengal from US and Canada on the point that the requirements are more elsewhere. In this manner Winston Churchill, his government and their selfish colonial policies caused the death of 3 million Bengalis and turned Bengal into a graveyard.

Pictures taken during the Bengal Famine of 1943

5

Activities in Far East

"My attack on Singapore was a bluff - a bluff that worked. I had 30,000 men and was outnumbered more than three to one. I knew that if I had to fight for long for Singapore, I would be beaten. That is why the surrender had to be at once."

- Tomoyuki Yamashita (Japanese Commander in Singapore)

It was one of the greatest military defeats that the British Army suffered which is known as the *fall of Singapore.* But before that we need to note that the Japanese troops began to capture the British occupied Malaya and Thiland in the month of December 1941 under their *Malyan Campaign.* The Japanese were highly interested in capturing the port city of Singapore within a short time as that particular place was of great strategic significance. The allied or the Commonwealth forces were not adequately equipped to prevent the advance of the Japanese, who moved swiftly through the jungles of Malaya and by the seaborne landings. On January 11, 1942 Kuala Lumpur fell into the hands of the Japanese and then the aim was Singapore.

Australian troops arriving in Singapore during the 2nd World War

Singapore was considered to be a major British military base in South East Asia. The Allied Forces had the British Indian army men and the armed forces from Australia. The Allied Forces had no idea about the strength of the Japanese troops at all. The Japanese onslaught through the Malay Peninsula took everybody by surprise. The main essence of the Japanese attack was their speed and they did not allow the Allied Forces any time to re-group. The British had predicted that the Japanese would attack from the sea and all the defenses were pointed towards the sea. The British Commander **General Percival** had no clue that the Japanese forces may attacked through the mangrove swamps of the Malay Peninsula and that was exactly the route the Japanese took. The Japanese commander **Yamashita** had around 30,000 men with him to capture Singapore. The attack was based on speed, ferocity and surprise. The Japanese troops also used bicycles to advance through the jungles with speed.

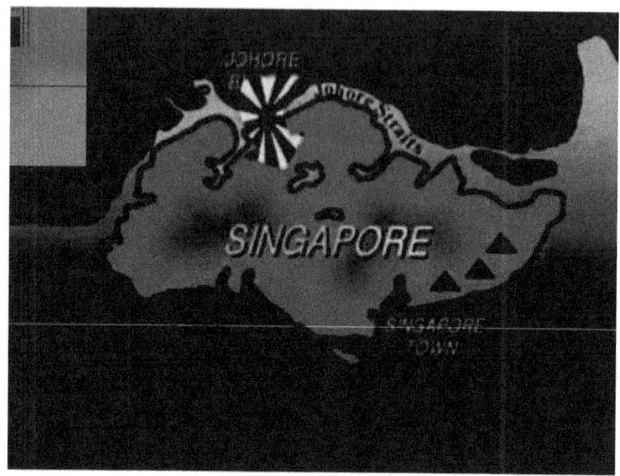

The Japanese attacked Singapore by crossing the Johore Straits

The Japanese commander took the advantage of the situation and pressed the Allied Forces to surrender. General Percival on the other hand, unaware of the Japanese strengths made the decision to surrender and on February 15, 1942 after hard fighting he called for ceasefire and unconditional surrender. Around 80,000 men of the allied forces were taken as *prisoners of war* by the Japanese.

Troops of the Allied Forces surrendered to the Japanese

The loss of Singapore sent shockwaves across the British Empire. The Japanese troops advanced around 600 miles in only fifty four days. During the Malayan Campaign the British, Australian and Indian forces suffered huge casualties and the remaining men were taken as prisoners of war. British Prime Minister **Winston Churchill** called the *fall of Singapore* to the Japanese the "worst disaster" and "largest capitulation" in British military history.

<u>6</u>

"The Land of Buddha"

India and Japan always enjoyed exchange of cultural, religious and philosophical ideas. India, the home of *Hinduism* and the birth place of *Buddha* had always been an attraction for Japan. India regarded Japan as an inspiration for their industrial development and for being an advancing Asian society. The victory of Japan over Russia in 1905 also infused inspiration among the Indian nationalists. Renowned cultural personalities of India and Japan like **Rabindranath Tagore** and **Okakura Tenshin** acknowledged the connection of the two Asian nations

and the vision of **Pan-Asianism.** At the end of 1ˢᵗ World War, Japan increasingly became a heaven for the Indian nationalists in exile, who were protected by the patriotic Japanese societies. Great nationalist and revolutionary **Rash Behari Bose** *was* among them, who became a very famous figure in Japan for his patriotism. Bose had cordial relationship with the Japanese authorities and with the help and support of the Japanese government he continued his fight against the colonial British for freedom of India in exile. Rash Bihari Bose was also the founder of the **Indian Independence League** which was an association of the freedom loving Indians living in South Asia and to work for Indian independence.

Indian revolutionary *Rash Behari Bose*
Was a leading figure of the *Gadar Revolution* which attempted
to trigger a mutiny in India against the colonial British
As a part of his revolutionary activities Bose attempted to
assassinate the Viceroy of India *Lord Hardinge* in 1912
After the failed attempt Bose took shelter in Japan and continued
his fight in exile for Indian independence throughout his life
He was the founder of the *Indian Independence League*
and also was the Head of the *Indian National Army* before
handing it over to *Netaji Subhas Chandra Bose*
Japanese Government honoured him with *"Order of the Rising Sun"*

At the very beginning of the war the Japanese authorities did not show any interest in India however, due to the repeated demands made by the Indians like Rash Behari Bose to support for Indian independence and to include this aspect under the Japanese campaign, Japan had to change its policies. The Japanese authorities also thought that this idea would be helpful for them in the coming days of the war. By the end of 1941, "India" started to feature prominently in Japanese policies. In various speeches made by **Prime Minister Tojo** in the **Diet** (the Japanese legislature) the matters related to Indian independence were mentioned. The military intelligence wing of the Japanese Imperial Army was engaged to work on this matter along with the Indian nationalists present in South East Asia. **Fujiwara Kikan** which was the name of a military intelligence operation established in Bangkok in 1941 by the Japanese Imperial Army HQ and its main task was intelligence gathering and contacting the important persons involved in Indian independence movement. The operation was headed by **Major Fujiwara Iwaichi.**

Major Fujiwara (left) greeting *Capt. Mohan Singh*
on the occasion of formation of the INA

Fujiwara came in contact of *Giani Pritam Singh* who was an Indian revolutionary and with Giani's help Fujiwara arranged a meeting with *Captain Mohan Singh.* Mohan Singh was a captain of the Punjab Regiment of the British Indian Army, who was taken as prisoner of war or POW by the Japanese troops during their invasion of Mayala. The Japanese authorities from the very beginning of their Malayan Campaign tried to separate the Indian soldiers from their British colleagues. Major Fujiwara asked Mohan Singh re-group the Indian POWs and take the charge of the unit. And, after that we see the creation of the concept of the *Indian National Army* or the *INA* under the leadership of Captain Mohan Singh in December 1941. Rash Behari Bose insisted that the new army should include not only the Indian POWs but also the Indian civilians of the South East Asia. Mohan Singh took the task of recruiting the volunteers for the INA and started visiting the Indian POW camps and meeting the Indian leaders living in various places of South East Asia.

On the other hand, after the fall of Singapore in February 1942 the Indian POWs were separated from their European colleagues and asked to gather at the **Farrer Park** or the Old Race Course field in Singapore on February 17, 1942. The crowd was first addressed by their British commander on that morning and he handed over the soldiers to the Japanese. The Indian men were full of anger and uncertainty after that announcement. But their mood completely changed when Major Fujiwara started addressing them and he termed the Indian soldiers as brothers and mentioned India as the ***"land of Buddha".*** He said that Japan does not consider them as prisoners and Japan wants India to become free as the people of India are struggling for their independence. Fujiwara urged the Indian soldiers to fight for the freedom of their motherland and he officially handed them over to Captain Mohan Singh, head of the INA. Then Mohan Singh started his address in Hindustani and asked the Indian men to join hands and join the INA and fight the colonial British for the sake of India's freedom. There were jubilations in the crowd and suddenly the defeated army got a new goal in life and that noble objective was to make their motherland free from the racist and cruel colonial rule. The entire crown was consisted of around 45,000 POWs and by the next day more than half of them joined the INA. That was the day when the INA was properly formed.

However, as the days passed the INA men felt

that the junior level Japanese armed forces were not treating them well and Mohan Singh was also not a person of high stature and a number of senior Indian army men were not happy to work under the command of Mohan Singh who was relatively junior to them. Many were of the opinion that the Japanese may treat them as puppets and may use them for achieving their own goals and a large section of the Indian men opined that they would go to the warfront if the *Indian National Congress* instructs them to do the same, although there was no direct connection between the INA and the Congress. Rash Behari Bose tried to manage the situation and tried to convince the Japanese authorities so that, **the INA was be governed by the *Indian Independence League (ILL)*, then the INA would be treated as an ally of the Japanese armed forces, after the independence of India, Japan would not have any territorial interest over India and the expenditure incurred by Japan in this process would be treated as a loan and the same would be repaid by India after her freedom, etc.** A resolution mentioning all these points were passed at a high level meeting held in Bangkok attended by Rash Behari Bose, the head of *ILL.* The situation improved a bit after that as the Japanese authorities issued proper instructions to the junior level forces. But the internal crisis continued which led to the arrest of Mohan Singh by the Japanese authorities. Rash Behari Bose ultimately had to take the responsibility to head the INA. But Rash Behari Bose himself, the officers of the INA and other Indian leaders of South East Asia were requesting the Japanese authorities to arrange to bring one man who had the charisma, the capacity, reputation and will to lead a real armed attack to eradicate the colonial masters out of India and that man .... was in Germany at that time.

Deshnayak Subhas

"One individual may die for an idea but that idea will after his death incarnate itself in a thousand lives"

- Netaji Subhas Chandra Bose

Subhas Chandra Bose the great son of India mentioned about a new philosophy, a new ethical conception in human affairs. A rare personality in contemporary world history, who was deeply involved in the great spiritual heritage of India and also actively concerned with the modern social and technological advancements in the world. His sense of mission did not admit any compromise or any reservation of any kind which makes him one of the most outstanding figures of the Indian national movement, who wanted to see India free and stated that a nation could be built by a genuine effort and uncompromised idealism.

Subhas Chandra Bose was born in January 23, 1897 in an affluent Bengali family in Cuttack, Odisha. His father *Janakinath Bose* was a famous lawyer and the name of his mother was *Prabhabati Devi*. Subhas came to Kolkata and was admitted to *Presidency College*. From his childhood days young

Subhas noticed the racist treatment which the

Subhas Chandra Bose (right) with Mahatma Gandhi

colonial British did towards the Indians. His nationalistic temperament came to light when he was expelled for assaulting Professor Oaten for his anti-India comments. Bose later completed his graduation from the *Scottish Church College* of Kolkata in 1918. In 1919 he visited London to prepare for the tough **Indian Civil Services** exams or to be more precise to fulfill his father's aspirations. Subhas Chandra qualified the exam with flying colours but did not accept the job and returned to India.

Bose joined the *Indian National Congress* in 1921 after returning to India. Subhas started assisting the famous freedom fighter *Deshbandhu Chittaranjan Das* who was an exponent of aggressive nationalism. During that time Bose came in contact of the revolutionaries and their secret organizations in Bengal. Subhas Bose was imprisoned a number of times for civil disobedience and his anti-British activities but his popularity as a mass leader reached new heights. As an important development, Bose tried to give the work of the revolutionaries a proper platform and a framework and in this way he formed the ***Bengal Volunteers Corps*** which was a revolutionary group to fight against the

A well known lawyer and great freedom fighter *Chittaranjana Das*
His contributions towards the freedom struggle
gave him the title of *Deshbandhu*
Subhas Chandra Bose regarded him as his *political guru*

British rule in India. Bose presented the group in the annual session of the Congress in Kolkata in 1928 under the leadership of *Major Satya Gupta* and declared himself as the *General Officer Commanding* or the *GOC* of the group. Many top Congress leaders including Mahatma Gandhi did not like the matter of formation of such a group and wearing military like uniforms (including Subhas as the *GOC*). But the aim of Bose was to provide a platform for the revolutionaries which must include a military like disciplined structure and wearing uniforms definitely had a symbolic importance. As a political milestone, Subhas Chandra Bose became the *President* of the all India youth wing of the Congress party, elected as the *Mayor* of the *Calcutta Municipal Corporation* and the *president* of the *Bengal Congress.* During 1930s Bose visited Europe and during his stay he held meetings with the Indian students and the European political leaders including *Benito Mussolini.* He also held meetings with the leaders of the *Labour Party* (including *Lord Clement Attlee*) during his visit England.

**Subhas Chandra Bose in uniform as the GOC
of the Bengal Volunteers Corps**

Subhas Bose got elected as the President of the Congress party in 1938 which was a major breakthrough in his political carrier. Subhas Chandra Bose had strong political opinion about the colonial government and advocated for **Purna Swaraj** or complete independence of India and no dominion status at all. He was of the opinion that the colonial masters were not going to grant independence to India and they have betrayed us during the 1st World War where they deployed Indian soldiers in the war fronts at various places of the globe. The Indian soldiers gave away their lives fighting on behalf of the British but in return Indians got nothing, rather their colonial atrocities increased as we had to witness massacres like the *"Jallianwala Bag"*. Subhas was also ready to use force to eradicate the colonial masters, which the top leaders of the Congress and Mahatma Gandhi opposed. But by then Bose had already became a leader of great stature in India and his popularity stated growing day by day. Importantly, *Gurudev Rabindranath Tagore* gave him the title of *"Deshnanak"* (leader of the nation) and Tagore also dedicated his famous book **Tasher Desh** in the name of Subhas Bose.

Bose as the President of the Indian National Congress

Subhas Bose was elected as president again in 1939 over Gandhiji's preferred candidate *Pattabhi Sitaramayya*, which created a situation of crisis within the Congress party. Bose was not even allowed to form his presidential cabinet and he was marginalized from the party by the other top leaders. Finally Bose had to resign from the party due to the differences of opinion. Subhas Chandra Bose founded the **Forward Bloc** in June 1939 as a new political entity and continued his political journey. The new political party organized massive anti-British political rallies in various places of India. At the outbreak

of the **2nd World War** Bose advocated for nationwide civil disobedience to protest against *Viceroy Lord Linlithgow's* decision to declare war on behalf of India without any consultation with the political setup of India. Subhas also failed to persuade the matter with Mahatma Gandhi and organized protests in Kolkata. Bose was then arrested by the authorities and following his hunger strike and ill health, he was shifted to his house in Kolkata and kept under house arrest and the Bengal CID was given the responsibility of surveillance.

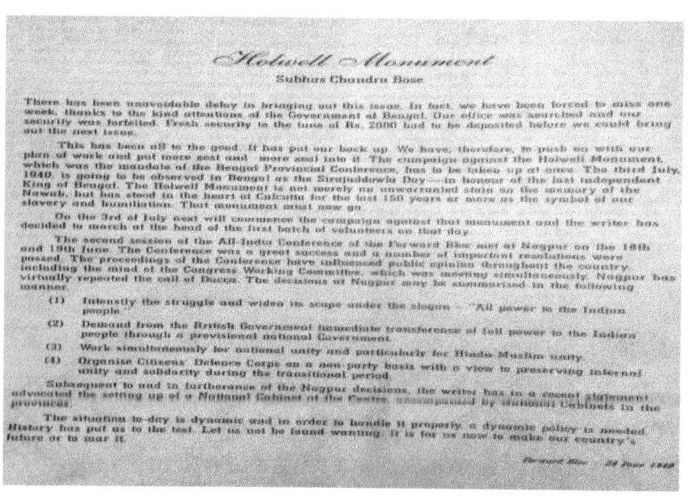

Holwell Monument

Subhas Chandra Bose

There has been unavoidable delay in bringing out this issue. In fact, we have been forced to miss one week, thanks to the kind attentions of the Government of Bengal. Our office was searched and our security was forfeited. Fresh security to the tune of Rs. 2000 had to be deposited before we could bring out the next issue.

This has been all to the good. It has put our back up. We have, therefore, to push on with our plan of work and put more zest and more zeal into it. The campaign against the Holwell Monument, which was the mandate of the Bengal Provincial Conference, has to be taken up at once. The third July, 1940, is going to be observed in Bengal as the Sirajuddowla Day—in honour of the last independent King of Bengal. The Holwell Monument is not merely an unwarranted stain on the memory of the Nawab, but has stood in the heart of Calcutta for the last 150 years or more as the symbol of our slavery and humiliation. That monument must now go.

On the 3rd of July next will commence the campaign against that monument and the writer has decided to march at the head of the first batch of volunteers on that day.

The second session of the All-India Conference of the Forward Bloc met at Nagpur on the 18th and 19th June. The Conference was a great success and a number of important resolutions were passed. The proceedings of the Conference have influenced public opinion throughout the country, including the mind of the Congress Working Committee, which was meeting simultaneously. Nagpur has virtually repeated the call of Dacca. The decisions at Nagpur may be summarised in the following manner.

(1) Intensify the struggle and widen its scope under the slogan — "All power to the Indian people."

(2) Demand from the British Government immediate transference of full power to the Indian people through a provisional national Government.

(3) Work simultaneously for national unity and particularly for Hindu-Muslim unity.

(4) Organise Citizens' Defence Corps on a non-party basis with a view to preserving internal unity and solidarity during the transitional period.

Subsequent to and in furtherance of the Nagpur decisions, the writer has in a recent statement advocated the setting up of a National Cabinet at the Centre, accompanied by National Cabinets in the provinces.

The situation to-day is dynamic and in order to handle it properly, a dynamic policy is needed. History has put us to the test. Let us not be found wanting. It is for us now to make our country's future or to mar it.

Forward Bloc — 24 June 1940

<u>8</u>
The Great Escape

"Life loses half its interest if there is no struggle- if there are no risks to be taken"

- Netaji Subhas Chandra Bose

Subhas was a man with unlimited love for his motherland and a man of unlimited courage and his entire life was an example of the same. Political marginalization and restrictions imposed by the British, nothing could stop him to continue his fight to make liberate India. He was impressed by the socialist ideas adopted by Russia and their technological and social developments. Subhas Chandra Bose was of the opinion that the colonial British cannot be trusted that they would grant independence to India in near future and that is why, it was right time during the world war to approach the anti-British nation like Russia for help to liberate. Being under house arrest, Bose planned for an escape and his destination was Russia or the Soviet Union. The people involved in this plan were his Forward Bloc colleague ***Akbar Shah*** and nephew ***Sisir Kumar Bose.*** On January 18, 1941 at 1.15 AM, Bose left his Elgin Road house along with Sisir Kumar Bose by dodging the police personnel of the Bengal CID. Sisir Bose accompanied Subhas Bose till *Gomoh* railway station of Bihar. Then he reached *Lahore* of present day Pakistan and finally reached *Peshawar*.

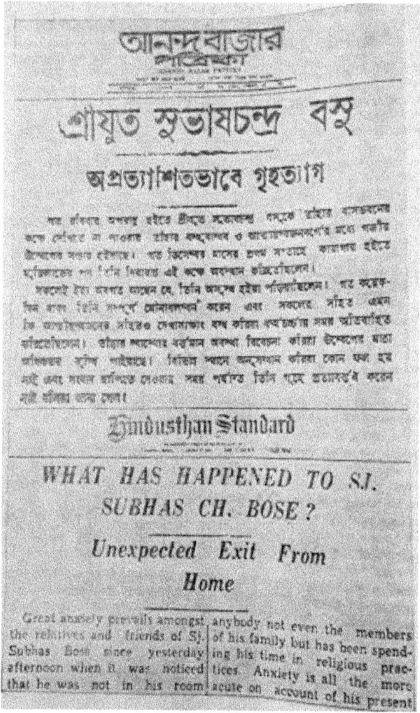

Anada Bazar Patrika and The Statesman reporting the disappearance of Subhas Chandra Bose

Now the next destination was *Kabul* and the way to Kabul was full of danger but it was impossible to restrict Bose in his mission. With the help of Akbar Shah and his friends of the *Kirti Kisan Party* , Bose was trained to appear as a *Pathan* and started his long journey on foot towards Kabul with *Bhagat Ram Talwar.* When he finally reached Kabul he tried to contact the Russian embassy but he was not successful. However, he could contact the *Italian* consulate in Kabul and they assured him that they would be able to help Bose. To Bose's surprise Russia was not ready to give shelter to him though they agreed to provide him a transit visa to reach *Berlin* via Russia. Italian consulate informed Subhas Bose that *Germany* showed some interest in this regard. Bose was disappointed as he was expecting that Russia or the Soviet Union would help him and forward assistance to liberate India. However, he thought about another opportunity that *Hitler's* Germany had an upper hand over the allied forces or the British forces and there were many Indian POWs arrested by the German forces and there may be a possibility that with the help of Germany a force may be created with the Indian POWs and that armed force may march through Russia and Afghanistan to attack India to defeat the British, as Britain was more engaged in the battle fields outside India.

Subhas Chandra Bose began his journey with the help of the Italian government with an Italian passport with the name *Orlando Mazzotta.* Then he reached *Moscow*, then to *Rome* and finally from Rome he was flown to Berlin by a special aircraft in the month of April 1941. One noteworthy point is that Subhas Bose had no sympathy for the Nazi Germany nor he ever advocated ***Adolf Hitler*** and his only intention was to eradicate the colonial British from India for that he was ready to take help by any foreign nation. The German government formed the *Special Bureau for India* which was a bureau established within the Information Department of the Foreign Office at the request of Subhas Chandra Bose and its main function was to aid Bose in his work.

Netaji (left) having a talk with the German officials

With the help of the bureau Bose came to the contact of some of Indians who voluntarily joined Bose. *Abid Hasan Safrani, Dr. Girija Mukherjee, A.C.N Nambiar, Pramod Sengupta* were prominent among these people. Then on the historic day of November 2, 1942 Subhas Bose established the *Free Indian Legion* or the **Free India Centre.** In the first meeting held on that day gave birth to three concepts **"Jai Hind", "Azad hind Zindabad"** and **"Netaji"**. From then Subhas Chandra Bose was known as *Netaji Subhas Chandra Bose*, as the term Netaji means *"the great leader"*. Netaji then established the **Azad Hind Radio** in Berlin from where he addressed his countrymen in India and Indians all around the world to unit and to fight against the colonial British. The British government could very well understand the possible threat and engaged their military intelligence wings to trace the activities of Netaji. Bose started visiting the Indian POW camps who were arrested by the Nazi Germany from the war-fronts of Africa. *Bose addressed them and asked them to join him and to forget the oath which they had taken in the name of the British Crown and to fight against the colonial power. He said that no other duty is as sacred as to fight for the freedom of your motherland and this sense of duty supersedes any oath taken in the name of any emperor of the world.* Bose was successful in making the Indian soldiers understand what he was trying to convey however, a small number of them actually joined him. The number increased as time progressed and Netaji established the **Azad Hind Fauj** with the Indian army men in Germany and took the guard of honour as the supremo along with the German representatives. This force along with the German army was about to march into India to defeat the British. Then finally Netaji got the opportunity to meet the dictator ***Adolf Hitler*** however, the meeting was not very fruitful as he expected. The said meeting was attended by two of the high profile officials of the Nazi government. *At the beginning after the introductions, Netaji was greeted by Hitler and he enquired about his stay at Berlin and about the progress of his works for the Free India Center. Netaji in return thanked him for the help and support provided to him by the German government. It is important to mention that although Hitler was against the British but he was of the opinion that British occupation in India was in favour of the Indians, as the Indians are* *incapable of governing themselves and he expressed his feelings in that meeting. He also said that India would not be able to achieve freedom even in next 150 years. Netaji politely but with a firm voice expressed that India had not lost its manhood, Indians have not mortgaged their spirits to the colonial masters and very soon India is going achieve her freedom. Hitler might not have*

Netaji shaking hands with Adolf Hitler

agreed with the statement of Netaji but he was impressed by his personality and understood his desperateness to make his motherland free from the foreign rule. Then the fuehrer showed Netaji a map and said that Germany would be able to march into India only when Soviet could be captured (this was surprising news for Netaji) and that would take at least two years. And, if Netaji was desperate for India's freedom then taking help from Japan would be a better idea. He also mentioned that reaching Japan by air would be risky and Netaji's life is valuable for them. Hitler said about talking to the Japanese and to plan for a submarine journey for Netaji. Bose lastly mentioned that the fuehrer was misinformed or he had misconceptions about India and *the Indians, which he had mentioned in his book **Mein Kampf**. He said that if the fuehrer may erase those lines from his book. Then Hitler firmly said that he kept those lines intentionally so that, the Germans never ever think of becoming slaves like the Indians. At the end of the meeting Hitler greeted Netaji 'a happy journey'.*

After the meeting Netaji could understand that he was not going to get any direct help from the Germans and his created Azad Hind Fauj would be of no use. Then he approached the Japanese consulate as a part of his next action plan. On the other hand in the Far East, Rash Behari Bose and top INA officials were requesting the Japanese authorities to bring Netaji to Japan. Rash Behari Bose contacted Netaji and invited him to Japan and to take the charge of IIL and INA. As Netaji came in contact of the Japanese consulate in Germany, the Japanese officials welcomed him and assured all kinds of assistance so that he may reach Tokyo. In the mean time Netaji handed over the responsibilities of the Azad Hind men to Nambier and had an arrangement with the Nazi government so that his men were looked after and they were not sent to any war-front by the Germens. Japan showed keen interest for transfer of Netaji by April 1942 but it took months for Germany to arrange the same. It was in the month of February 1943, when Netaji started his momentous submarine journey with *Abid Hasan Safrani*. The information regarding the journey was kept secret, even Abid Hasan had no idea about the same. The submarine journey was very tough especially for a civilian and that too during the dangerous time of the world war. However, Netaji did not waste time and during the three months journey time he dictated the future speeches to Abid Hasan that he was about to deliver. The critical time came when the voyage arrived near *Madagascar* and a Japanese submarine was waiting to receive Netaji. But there was a sea storm and due to the high waves of the Indian Ocean the two submarines could not come closure. The German submarine captain recommended Netaji to go back as this was full of life risk for Netaji. But Netaji replied him that *"Captain, I have not come all this way just to go back"*. Bose and Hasan got into a rubber dinghy and paddled through the sea waves and finally reached the Japanese submarine. That event was a unique example of submarine to submarine transfer of civilians during the Second World War. On the Japanese submarine Netaji and Hasan received warm welcome as if it was home coming for them. Then they reached *Sumatra* and from there Netaji travelled to *Tokyo* by air.

Although finally Netaji reached Tokyo but there was substantial delay. As per historian Gen. G.D Bakshi, invasion of India with the help of Japan could have been easier if Netaji could reach the Far East by mid of 1942, when the momentum was with the Japanese after the fall of Malaya and Singapore. As by 1943 the allied forces stated taking upper hand.

<u>9</u>

Arzi Hukumat E Azad Hind
(Govt. of Free India)

"The British know very well that I say what I mean and that I mean what I say, so when I say war, I mean war, war to the finish, war that only end in the freedom of India"

- Netaji Subhas Chandra Bose

-

Rash Behari Bose and Netaji met for the first time at the Imperial Hotel in Tokyo. That was an emotional moment for the two great sons of Bengal and they discussed about the future planning and activities. On June 10, 1943 Netaji met **Hideki Tojo**, the Japanese Prime Minister. Netaji received a warm welcome from Prime Minister Tojo. Netaji till that time became a big political figure not only in the political sphere of Japan but in entire South Asia. As he was not only the former President of the *Indian National Congress* but a person of great courage and political will who had already impressed the Italians and the Nazi Germans. The German foreign minister himself got highly influenced by Netaji's persona and helped him to form the *Free India Center* and even arrange a meeting with Hitler. Prime Minister Tojo was also very much impressed by the magnanimous personality of Netaji and assured him to provide all kinds of assistance for India's independence. On June 12, 1943 *Tokyo Radio* announced the presence of Netaji in Japan. Prime Minister Tojo declared about Japan's commitment to help Subhas Bose to achieve India's freedom in the Japanese legislature. Netaji then held a series of meetings with the Japanese top officials and briefed the press about the overall future activities. He extended his support to the *Quit India Movement* declared by the Congress in India and mentioned the press that the same needed to be escalated as an armed struggle. He stated *"only when the Indian people have received their baptism by fire on a large scale, will they be qualified to achieve freedom."* Netaji then addressed the people of Indian origin in Japan, Singapore, Malaya and of the entire South East Asia to get ready to begin a mammoth fight against the British for the sake of independence of India.

Netaji briefing the Japanese officials in Tokyo

On June 27, 1943 Netaji arrived in Singapore and he was accompanied by Rash Behari Bose. Netaji was welcomed like a hero by the members of the INA and the Indian diaspora who were eagerly waiting for his arrival for months. Thousands of people gathered just to get a glimpse of the great man and he was like a Messiah for them. People shouted slogans *'Netaji Subhas Chndra Bose ki jai'* and the INA band sang the famous song composed by them *'Subhas ji, Subhas ji wo jane Hind agaye'.* On July 4, 1943 at the *Cathey Cinema Hall* which was then the tallest building in Singapore a meeting was organized, which was attended by the INA officials men and thousands of Indians from various places of South East Asia. During that meeting Rash Behari Bose formally introduced Netaji and stated that *"I have brought for you one of the best specimen of an India, Subhas Chandra Bose"* and he officially handed over the charge of both *Indian Independence League* and the *Indian National Army* to Netaji. And, then Netaji addressed, he said that the road to freedom would be full of pain and troubles but it was certain that India shall be free. Now the INA men were sure that they had got the true leader who was fearless, person of great stature, high repute and having the will to lead them to the freedom of India. On the next day at the *Singapore City Hall ground* Netaji reviewed the march past by the 1500 INA soldiers led by the INA military chief *Maj. Gen. Kiani.* The Japanese Prime Minister *Tojo* was present in the event as the Guest of Honour. The famous slogan of *"Chalo Dilli"* or *onwards to Delhi* was given by Netaji during his address and he said the historic *Red Fort* of Delhi would be their final destination, which became the war cry of the INA. Netaji also renamed the INA as the *Azard Hind Fauj* which he had already formed during his stay in Germany. After that Netaji addressed many gatherings at various places of South East Asia. He travelled to *Rangoon, Penag, Bangkok* and *Saigon* and received great receptions by the Indians. Netaji emphasized that INA should be a true Indian force and common Indians of South East Asia must join. He decided not to be fully dependent upon the Japanese help and he started raising funds for the INA from the people of Indian origin. The famous slogan of Netaji ***"Give me blood and I shall give you freedom"*** changed the lives of many Indians who not even for once visited India and now they were ready to donate everything they have for the cause of the freedom of their motherland 'India'. Thousands of Indians also joined the INA and got trained to fight the colonial British. Netaji urged the Indian women to join the INA and they should not refrain from fighting the enemy. The Japanese army officials initially made some objections to this but those could not stand in front of Netaji's decision. Netaji decided to create an *all-women* regiment in the name of the great warrior Queen of Jhansi ***'Lakshmi Bai'*** who sacrificed her life fighting the British during the 1857 uprising in India. *Capt. (Dr.) Lakshmi Swaminathan* of the INA was given the responsibility to form the regiment. Netaji also decided that the expenditure to be incurred for the women's regiment would be taken care by the funds raised by the INA and Japanese help would not be taken. *This was probably for the first time in the history of warfare in the entire world that an all-women regiment was made and they were trained to truly fight on the battle field.*

Aufruf Boses an die Legion
Bose's message to the Indian Legion
Rangoon, 7. 1. 1944

(Übersetzung)

Soldaten der indischen Legion in Europa! Ich freue mich, diesen Aufruf von Burma aus an Euch richten zu können. Ich möchte Euch Gelegenheit geben, meine grosse Freude, mit Euren Kameraden der indischen Nationalarmee in Burma zusammen sein zu können, mit mir zu teilen. Vom heutigen Tage an werde ich mich ganz der Leitung und Fortsetzung unseres heiligen Kampfes bis zum siegreichen Einmarsch in Delhi, und bis der letzte Engländer vom indischen Boden vertrieben ist, widmen. In den vergangenen sechs Monaten habe ich keine Mühe gescheut, die drei Millionen Inder in Ostasien in den Plan der totalen Mobilisation einzubeziehen. Heute stehen 3 Millionen unserer Landsleute alt und jung, Mann, Frau und Kind wie ein Wall aus Granit hinter Euren Waffenkameraden in Ostasien. Sie bilden im wahrsten Sinne des Wortes eine Heimatfront, auch wenn wir unseren Feldzug von aussen her durchführen müssen. Genau wie Eure Waffenkameraden in Ostasien sollt Ihr fühlen, dass das gesamte indische Volk in und ausserhalb der Heimat hinter Euch steht. Das neue Jahr stellt uns vor gewaltige Aufgaben. Ich bin der Vorsehung dankbar, dass mein lang gehegter und glühender Wunsch, am Neujahrstage auf indischem Boden zu stehen, sich nun erfüllt hat. Am ersten dieses Monats erhielt ich die Nachricht, dass unsere Soldaten tatsächlich indischen Boden betreten haben. Diese Nachricht hat wie ein Lauffeuer die Herzen unserer Soldaten erfasst, und diejenigen, die aus verschiedenen Gründen noch hinter der Front liegen, drängen zum Vormarsch. Die Stunde der Bewährung hat jedoch noch nicht geschlagen. Ihr müsst auf alles gefasst sein.

Ich bin fest überzeugt, dass Ihr und Eure Kameraden Euch durch nichts von Eurem Wege abbringen lasst; denn der Kampf, den Ihr führt, ist gerecht, und Ihr müsst Eure Aufgabe erfüllen. Es ist Eure Pflicht, Euch als Soldaten der indischen Nationaarmee in Europa den Briten zur Wehr zu setzen, wo immer Ihr sie treffen mögt. Ich bin stolz auf Euch, dass Ihr Eure Pflicht bis zum Letzten tut und damit die Ehre Indiens hoch haltet. Möge die Vorsehung mir bald die Gelegenheit geben, Euch als siegreiche indische Nationalarmee in Europa auf freiem indischen Boden willkommen heissen zu können.

Inquilab Zindabad! — Azad Hind Zindabad!
Es lebe die Revolution! — Es lebe ein freies Indien!
gezeichnet
SUBHAS CHANDRA BOSE.

(Original)

Soldiers of the Indian Legion in Europe! I am glad to issue this appeal to you from Burma. I want to give you the opportunity to share with me the immense joy I feel now to be in Burma with your comrades of the Indian National Army. From to-day onwards I shall devote myself entirely to the directing and continuing of our holy struggle until our victorious entry into Delhi and until the last Englishman has been driven off Indian soil. In these past six months I have spared no effort to draw the 3 million Indians living in East Asia into the scheme of total mobilization. To-day the 3 million countrymen of ours young and old, man, woman and child, stand like a wall of granite behind your comrades-in-arms in East Asia. They form in the truest sense of the word a home front even though we have to carry out our campaign from outside. Just like your comrades-in-arms in East Asia, you too must feel that the entire Indian people within and without your country stand behind you. This new year finds us facing big problems. I am thankful to Providence that my ardent hope which I have repeatedly expressed, to stand on Indian soil on New Year's Day has been realized. On the first of this month I received the news that our soldiers have really set foot on Indian soil. This news has caught the hearts of our soldiers like a flame, and those, who for various reasons are behind the front are straining to march forward. The hour of trial, however, has not passed yet. You must be prepared for everything.

I am convinced that you and your comrades will never allow yourselves to be diverted from your chosen path, because the struggle you are carrying on is just and you have to fulfill your task. It is your duty as soldiers of the Indian National Army in Europe to oppose the British, wherever you meet them. I am proud of you that you are fulfilling your duty to the fullest satisfaction and are thereby keeping high the honour of India. May Providence give me the opportunity soon to welcome you on Indian soil as the victorious Indian National Army of Europe.

Inquilab Zindabad!
Azad Hind Zindabad!
signed
SUBHAS CHANDRA BOSE.

Netaji's message in the Azad Hind monthly news paper

Netaji addressing the Indians in Singapore

On the historic day of 21st October 1942 Netaji proclaimed the ***Arzi Hukumat E Azad Hind*** or the ***Provisional Government of Free India*** in exile (this was a provisional govt. as a permanent Indian government could only be established by the people of India when India becomes independent). Netaji took the oath in front of a huge gathering in Singapore as the *Prime Minister* and *Head of the State*. As Netaji took the oath *"In the name of God, I take this sacred oath to liberate India and four hundred million of my countrymen"* his voice chocked out of emotion but he continued *"I, Subhas Chandra Bose, will continue the sacred war of freedom till the last breath of my life"*. This was a red letter day in the history of India and especially in the history of Indian freedom struggle. The government created their own civic code, it had issued postage stamps and it also established a bank known as 'Azad Hind Bank', which also issued currency notes. 'Hindustani' was adopted as the official language by the provisional government. The simplified

Hindustani version of the song *Jana Gana Mana* by *Rabindranath Tagore* which is *Shubh Sukh Chain* was adopted as the national anthem. The government was recognized by Japan, Germany, Italy and other axis power nations. Netaji received a congratulatory note from Ireland. Though the Soviet officially did not make any announcements to recognize the Azad Hind Govt. however, the Azad Hind govt. had a consulate office in the Soviet and by studying the declassified documents this may be easily understood that Netaji maintained cordial relationship with the Soviet Union. Prime Minister Tojo gave the territorial authority of the Japanese captured Indian territories of Andaman and Nicobar to Netaji Subhas Chandra Bose.

On October 23, 1943 the provisional government of Azad Hind declared war on Britain and America at five minutes past mid night. *"The British know very well that I say what I mean and that I mean what I say, so when I say war, I mean war, war to the finish, war that only end in the freedom of India"*. The war of independence had begun.

War of Independence

"India is calling. Blood is calling to blood. Getup, we have no time to lose. Take up your arms. The road to Delhi is the road to freedom. Chalo Delhi"

\-   Netaji Subhas Chandra Bose

Singapore was roaring with the slogans of *Jai Hind* and *Chalo Dilli* and all the Indians were charged up for a massive fight. The INA was mainly divided in three divisions and there were brigades within those divisions to launch guerilla warfare, namely, *Gandhi Brigade, Nehru Brigade, Azad Brigade and Subhas Brigade.* As per the official history of the INA the total strength of the INA was 60,000. The Supreme Commander of the INA, Netaji Subhas Chandra Bose decided to launch the war through the Indo-Barma border and that is why, he shifted his head quarters from Singapore to Rangoon. *Netaji was very clear about the role of the INA and before beginning of the INA advance, he made a final deal with the Japanese authorities that they would have no authority over the INA and the INA would have full control over the areas of India which would be captured by the INA. Only Indian tricolor would be hoisted in those areas and the Japanese forces role would be restricted to help the INA after entering into India.*

It is important to mention that at that point of time the allied forces gathered good strength, they were now quite aware about the Japanese tactics and after the U.S joined the war the allied forces achieved air superiority over the Japanese. Historian Gen. G.D Bakshi explained that if Japan could have managed to bring Netaji from Germany at the beginning of 1942 when the Japanese had the upper hand, the situation could have been totally different. And, due to this delay the allied forces got sufficient time to regroup and made solid strategies to restrict a potential threat from the Indo- Burma border.

The limitless courage and will of their Supreme Commander was the main asset of the INA men. They did not have any air force, for that they were totally dependent on the Japanese air force. They did not have sophisticated weapons, no adequate transport facilities and not even sufficient food or medicine. However, they were ready to sacrifice their lives in the name of their supreme leader and for the freedom of India. The INA achieved its first military success on February 4, 1944 in the *Arakan Hills* of Burma. Netaji congratulated his man and he shifted his office near the Indian border. The INA and the Japanese forces advanced towards Imphal. The main problems they faced, was not the enemy but the monsoon rains which destroyed the roads and it became impossible to send reinforcements, food and medicine. But the INA men fought bravely and on 8th April they captured Kohima and *on April 14, 1944 the Azad Hind Fauj or the INA reached* **Moirang** *in Manipur and for the first time the Indian tricolor flattered on an Indian territory.* And, now the aim was to capture Imphal and the rail head quarters of Dimapur. But the continued rains caused huge damage and there was a total stoppage of supply of food and medicines due to logistical issues. The problems caused by malaria and insect bites in the jungles were becoming impossible to handle. On the other hand, the strong British-Indian and American forces with modern equipments and superior air power stopped the advance of the Japanese- INA forces. But the resistance shown by the Japanese-INA forces was exemplary. The INA held their positions for three months though there was no food, no medicine and they were dying one by one out of starvation, malaria and other diseases, which allowed the Japanese to fight a fierce battle with the allied forces. This battle saw a series of attacks and counter attacks, instances of hand to hand fight but ultimately it was the air power of the allied forces and poor logistical supports of the Japanese-INA forces which cost them and there was no other way other than to retreat. The Japanese-INA forces suffered huge casualties in this battle of Imphal and Kohima. According to historian *Ranjan Borra, "the Imphal Campaign (including the battle of Kohima) will perhaps go down in the history as one of the most daring and disastrous campaign in the* *annals of world history."*

After the retreat, the INA men were devastated but still they believed that they could achieve their goal under the leadership of Netaji. Who stated that this was only a temporary setback and we lost the battle due to the monsoon weathers and raised the spirits of his shaken men. *He said that the independence of India would be an outcome, whoever wins or loses the war, India would be free.* Bose continued his fight and started deputing his officials as ambassadors of the Azad Hind Govt. to various Axis Power nations with the help of Japan to have greater legitimacy to his government. The INA men were highly upset with the Japanese forces as they treated the Indians during the Battle of Kohima and complained for not providing logistical support. The Japanese forces were of the opinion that the INA men were not capable enough to fight but they could not make any serious objections due to the high prestige of Netaji. In the meantime, PM Tojo resigned from his position and Rash Behari Basu died. Bose went to Tokyo to meet the new PM and reiterated that the Azad Hind Govt. must be respected as a sovereign power and arrangement for proper food and logistics must be done for the INA men. The demands of Netaji were accepted.

Rangoon was becoming dangerous for Netaji to stay due to the air bombings of the allied forces who were marching towards Rangoon. The Japanese started living Rangoon. Netaji decided to stay at Rangoon and did not fear for his life but the higher officials of the INA continuously insisted him to leave for *Mowlamyine* which was relatively safer, as his life was precious for liberation of India. After that, Netaji accepted their request. Then one division of the INA alone stationed at Rangoon for its protection and others got ready for the war against the advancing British-Indian-American forces on the *Mount Popa* and *Mektila.* In these famous battles, there were better coordination between both the Japanese and the INA forces. But like the battle of Kohima due to the superior air power finally the British won the battle though the Japanese- INA forces fought bravely. Netaji was still determined that he would stay in Burma and try to enter India again through guerrilla warfare, because if the Indians could be made aware about their heroics and if somehow he gets the chance to enter into India that might propagate in a nationwide revolt against the British. However, for this to happen he required the assistance of the *Burmese Liberation Army (BNA),* which was fighting against the British, with Japanese. But *Aung San* the chief of the BNA had switched sides and started attacking the Japanese. Aung San assured Netaji for whom he had great respect that his men would never attack the INA, as he was well aware that Netaji and his men were fighting for the liberation of India and nothing else. But Netaji's last attempt to fight was also shuttered with this. Ultimately Netaji had to leave Rangoon on April 24, 1945 and had to move towards Bangkok but he did not go there on his car, rather he went on foot along with his INA men and the women's regiment. They finally reached there on May 14, 1945 and it was a very tiring journey which was full of danger and Netaji and his men somehow survived the enemy bombing. From Bangkok Netaji flew to Singapore, where he stayed till August 1945.

A photo of the surrendered INA men at *Mount Popa*

After the atomic blasts in the Japanese cities of Hiroshima and Nagasaki, Japan declared its surrender on August 15, 1945 and it was all over for Netaji and the INA. Netaji had a meeting with his officials for making arrangements to pay the dues to the INA men and to build a War Memorial for the Azad Hind Fouj, so that people could remember their fight and sacrifices. The war memorial was erected within a very short time before the British force's advance in Singapore. Studies state that Netaji was egger to talk to the Japanese authorities to consult on weather the INA would surrender with the Japanese or not and he had plans to move towards Tokyo for that. Studies also suggest that in consultation with the Japanese intelligence agencies Netaji had the plan to move to the Soviet and fight for India's freedom from there and he wanted to move towards Manchuria. And, in the mid of August he left Singapore for Saigon then to may be Tokyo or Manchuria but that is said to be the last journey of *Netaji Subhas Chandra Bose*.

The INA war memorial destroyed by the British forces in Singapore in 1945 at the orders of Lord Mountbatten, the last Viceroy of India

A plaque erected by the *National Heritage Board* of Singapore in memory of the INA men at the same site where the former INA war memorial was built.

"I appeal to you to cherish the same optimism as myself and to believe like myself that the darkest hour always precedes the dawn. India shall be free and before long"

-Netaji Subhas Chandra Bose

Netaji's prophecy proved to be correct in many ways. During the war he said that whoever wins the war but after the war India would be free. He had also stated earlier that the colonial powers would not be able to keep India in bondage for long. Netaji believed that the Indians would revolt against the British when they would be aware about the sacrifices made by his men. Surprisingly, all the above prophecies made by him actually happened within a short period after the end of the war. We have already discussed about the revolts during the *Red Fort Trials* and the announcement made by PM Clement Attlee for granting independence to India.

During the Second World War the people of India did not get the chance to listen to the radio broadcasts of Netaji, both from Germany or from the Far East. The media was not allowed to cover the updates of the Azad Hind Fauj or the lectures of Netaji. Nobody in India were aware about the formation of the Azad Hind Govt. and the great contributions made by the Indians leaving in South East Asia to liberate India. During the Battle of Kohima, the British authorities and the British influenced media in India propagated that they were only fighting the Japanese who were trying to invade India but nowhere had they mentioned about the INA. The Indian members of the British Indian Army were also not aware that along with the Japanese they were about to fight with their own men, who were fighting to liberate their motherland. *Dr. Satyendra Basu,* the former INA officer writes that when their unit was arrested by the British in Rangoon and they were kept in jail, they were termed as 'JIFC' or *'Japanese Inspired Fifth Columnist'* and this was nothing but a British propaganda to humiliate them and so that the aspect of their freedom struggle was totally erased. The Redford Trails were also designed to prove that the INA members were traitors.

Netaji was a great statesman and his patriotism can never be disputed. He had great plans for nation building. He had displayed great skills in political leadership, international relations, diplomacy and military leadership. He made his army which was not based on any cast, language or religion like the traditional British Indian Army regiments. All his army units had members from all communities. Another important aspect which needs to be stated that though there were political differences between Bose and Gandhiji and between Bose and Pandit Jawaharlal Nehru but there are instances that they had immense respect for each other. Netaji named his brigades in the name of Gandhi, Nehru and Azad. He supported the call for Quit India by Mahatma Gandhi through his radio address from Berlin, he was the first person to call Mahatma Gandhi as *'the father of the nation'*. Gandhiji did not support the idea of use of force but told Netaji that if he could liberate India with his means then Gandhiji would be the first person to congratulate him. Mahatma Gandhi named Netaji as 'the patriot of the patriots'. After receiving the news of the plane crash, Gandhiji did not be believe that Netaji was no more and he sent a telegram to the Bose family in Kolkata advising them not to hold the *Shraddha* for Subhas. Pt. Nehru on the other hand, was one of the members of the group of lawyers which defended the INA soldiers during the Red Fort Trials. Pt. Nehru at the end of his first Independence Day address at the Red Fort shouted the famous slogan of the INA *'Jai Hind'* and after that every Indian prime minister does the same on this auspicious day during their address.

Eminent writer *Vivekananda Mukhopadhyay* stated that the Azad Hind Govt. was said to be a 'provisional' one, as the permanent govt. of Free Indian could only be formed by the people of India, when she would become free. It is true that Netaji took the help of a ruthless dictator like Adolf Hitler and also fought along with the Imperial Japan but that was only to liberate his motherland and that was a part of a diplomatic step which countries of earlier times and in modern days do to defeat the enemy (taking foreign help). The 200 years old British Raj was no less cruel than that of the Germany during Hitler's regime. So if we could negotiate with them for years after years and if the colonial masters could continue their atrocities (like the man-made *Bengal Famine of 1943*, which alone took the lives of around 3 million poor Indians,) then that makes the Empire, the ruler of India for centuries, a lot more dangerous than Germany during Hitler and the Imperial Japan (countries which traditionally having good relations with India from the ancient times).

On December 14, 1973 *Dr. M.C Widemann* Head of the Department of the South Asian Relations Research Department of the *Humboldt University, Berlin* in a press meet in Kolkata briefed the press. There he stated that in the democratic and republican Germany there were detailed studies related to Subhas Chandra Bose. The studies reveal that Netaji travelled to Germany with the intention to strengthen the Indian freedom movement. He also said that the Nazi Germany tried to use Netaji for own benefit but they failed. Nazi Germany also tried to deploy the Azad Hind Fauj men to fight against the Soviet however, Netaji's men rejected those proposals and later had to face trials for the same. Dr. M.C Widemann *also stated that* Netaji never became puppet in the hands of the

Nazi Germany. Again in the Far East, in December 1944 according to Maj. Gen. G.D Bakshi, when the Japanese envoy reached Rangoon without proper ambassadorial credentials, Netaji refused to receive him. When Netaji decided to raise the women's regiment, then the Japanese officials objected but those objections could not stand in front of Netaji's high esteem. The expenditures related to this regiment were also taken care by the INA funds and Japanese help was not taken. All these events state that Netaji never allowed both the Germans and the Japanese to use him or his men for their benefit and made them bound to treat the Azad Hind as their allies. I would like to end this book with the statements made by *Dr. Alexander Werth* who was a former official of the department of foreign ministry under the Nazi Germany. While analyzing the role of Netaji Subhas Chandra Bose and his relationship with the Axis Power nations during the Second World War, he stated that *"Regardless of the fact that he was operating in Axis countries in 1941-1945 Subhas Chandra Bose remained an uncompromising fighter for Indian Independence and- what is more – he continued to be a planer and builder of the free India of his dreams. The Axis Powers lost the war, but Subhas Chandra Bose won the victory of India over Britain and his ideas of national reconstruction will win many more victories in the days to come."*

*We salute the Supreme Commander of the Azad Hind
Fauj, the fighter and the Liberator of India
Netaji Subhas Chandra Bose*

BIBLIOGRAPHY

1) S.C Bose- 'The Indian Struggle' – Asian Publishing House, Bombay 1970.
2) S.C Bose- 'Crossroads' - Asian Publishing House, Bombay 1970.
3) S Bose- 'Patraboli' (Bengali)- M.S Sarkar and Sons Pvt. Ltd., Kolkata.
4) S.C Bose- 'Tanmer Swapna' (Bengali)- Annada Publishers Pvt. Ltd., Kolkata 1967.
5) V. Mukhopadhyay- 'Dwitiyo Mahajuddher Itihas' (Bengali)- Nabapatra Prakashan, Kolkata.
6) Gen. G.D Bakshi- 'Bose An Indian Samurai'- KW Publishers Pvt. Ltd., New Delhi.
7) Dr. Narayan Chandra- 'Subhas Chandra Bose The Pioneer Nation Builder'- Manna Publication, Kolkata.
8) S.K Bose- 'Netaji and Indian Freedom Proceedings'- Orient Longman Ltd., New Delhi 1973.
9) Chitra Basu –'Bharatiya Biplaber Bharatiya Path' (Bengali)- Loknath Prakashani, Kolkata.
10) S.K Bose –'Anirban Jyoti' (Bengali)- Dey's Publishing, Kolkata.
11) 'Paschimbanga' Magazine (Bengali)- Netaji Edition, Kolkata.
12) 'historic-uk.com' website blogs.
13) Articles of 'The Guardian' (website).
14) Wikipedia and Encyclopedia Britannica.
15) Statements made by Gen. G.D Bakshi and historian *Prof. Makkhan Lal* on various T.V shows regarding Netaji's contributions, on relations be-

tween Netaji and Mahatma Gandhi and on reasons for Netaji's exit from the Congress party.